Level F • Book 3

QuickReads®
A Research-Based Fluency Program

Elfrieda H. Hiebert, Ph.D.

MODERN CURRICULUM PRESS

Pearson Learning Group

Program Reviewers and Consultants

Dr. Barbara A. Baird
Director of Federal Programs/Richardson ISD
Richardson, TX

Dr. Kate Kinsella
Dept. of Secondary Education and Step to College Program
San Francisco State University
San Francisco, CA

Pat Sears
Early Child Coordinator/Virginia Beach Public Schools
Virginia Beach, VA

Dr. Judith B. Smith
Supervisor of ESOL and World and Classical Languages/Baltimore City Public Schools
Baltimore, MD

The following people have contributed to the development of this program:

Art and Design: Kathleen Ellison, Denise Ingrassia, Salita Mehta, Dan Thomas, Dan Trush

Editorial: Lynn W. Kloss

Marketing: Alison Bruno

Production/Manufacturing: Louis Campos, Michele Uhl

Publishing Operations: Jennifer Van Der Heide

ISBN 0-7652-7210-5

Printed in the United States of America

2 3 4 5 6 7 8 9 10   09 08 07 06

1-800-321-3106
www.pearsonlearning.com

Contents

Contents

SOCIAL
STUDIES

World War II

Contents

SCIENCE **Constructing a Building**

Contents

Acknowledgments

All photography © Pearson Education, Inc. (PEI) unless otherwise specifically noted.

Google™ is a trademark of Google, Inc.

Lycos® is a registered trademark of Carnegie Mellon University in the United States and other countries.

Cover: Markku Ulander/Lehtikuva/WireImage. 3: Private Collection, Archives Charmet/The Bridgeman Art Library. 4: © Bettmann/Corbis. 5: © Bettmann/Corbis. 6: National Geographic Image Collection. 7: © Dennis MacDonald/PhotoEdit. 8: © Ed Bock/Corbis. 10: Private Collection, Archives Charmet/The Bridgeman Art Library. 12: © Mimmo Jodice/Corbis. 14: © Ruggero Vanni/Corbis. 16: Mike Hewitt/Getty Images, Inc. 18: British Museum, London, UK/The Bridgeman Art Library. 24: © Bettmann/Corbis. 26: © Bettmann/Corbis. 28: AP/Wide World Photo. 30: © Bettmann/Corbis. 32: New York Times/Getty Images, Inc. 38: © Hulton-Deutsch Collection/Corbis. 40: Time Life Pictures/National Archives/Getty Images, Inc. 42: © Bettmann/Corbis. 44: © Bettmann/Corbis. 46: *l*. Hulton Archive Photos/Getty Images, Inc.; *r*. Hulton Archive Photos/Getty Images, Inc. 52: © David Young-Wolff/PhotoEdit. 54: *t*. National Geographic Image Collection; *b*. Tim Ridley, © DK Images, Courtesy of the Jane Goodall Institute, Clarendon Park, Hampshire. 56: © Corbis. 58: © Will Hart/PhotoEdit. 60: Dietmar Nill/Nature Picture Library. 66: *l*. Mark Gibson/Index Stock Imagery, Inc.; *r*. Library of Congress Photoduplication Service. 68: © Dennis MacDonald/PhotoEdit. 70: © Dennis MacDonald/PhotoEdit. 74: © Ulrike Welsch/PhotoEdit. 80: © Ed Bock/Corbis. 82: © Michael Newman/PhotoEdit. 84: SMART Technologies Inc. 86: © David Young-Wolff/PhotoEdit. 88: © Jose Luis Pelaez, Inc./Corbis.

Ancient Greece

In ancient Greece, people gathered to hear stories and discuss the news of the day.

The Ideas of Ancient Greece

Greece is a country in southern Europe. Greece is also the country in which the Olympics began. When the first[25] Olympic Games were held, more than 2,500 years ago, the Greek people already had a thriving culture. This culture is called ancient Greece.

Ancient Greece[50] is often called "the birthplace of the Western world." That is because the ideas of the ancient Greeks influenced the countries of Europe and North[75] America. Ancient Greece was the first nation to allow citizens to vote for their government.

In ancient Greece, only certain people were citizens. However, until[100] that time, no government had been determined by the votes of any of its people. The word *democracy* comes from the Greek words for *people*[125] and *rule*.

Today, many nations have a democratic government like the one the ancient Greeks created. In addition, nations around the world take part in the Olympics.[152]

Ancient Greece

This statue shows the Greek god Atlas carrying the world on his back.

Greek Myths

The ancient Greeks believed that gods and goddesses made and ruled the world. Ancient Greek writers and poets wrote stories about these gods[25] and goddesses. As the years passed, though, fewer people believed the stories. Yet people continued to enjoy hearing about gods and goddesses. Today, these stories[50] are known by the Greek word *myth*, which means "story."

One character in Greek myths was Atlas. Atlas was the strongest of the losers in[75] a big battle. After the battle, Atlas was punished by having to carry the world on his back. Sometimes, a person is described as being[100] "as strong as Atlas" or as "having the burdens of Atlas." *Atlas* is also the name both of a book of maps and of the[125] first bone in the back, which holds up the head. Many words in English, such as *giant* and *fate*, come from characters in Greek myths.[150]

Ancient Greece

This painting shows the king in the *Odyssey* as he was on his journey home.

Greek Classics

The literature of the ancient Greeks and Romans is often called the classics, meaning that they are models for writing that came later. Homer was the most famous ancient Greek writer. Homer's poems, the *Iliad* and the *Odyssey*, are classics. Both the *Iliad* and the *Odyssey* include myths about how the gods and goddesses were believed to help or harm people.

The *Iliad* tells about the disasters that happened to a warrior during the last year of a ten-year war that was fought over the city of Troy. The *Odyssey* tells about a Greek king's journey home after the war with Troy. Because he faced many problems along the way, the journey took the king ten years.

Homer's poems are so famous that their titles are often used to describe certain events. A series of disasters is sometimes called an *iliad*. A long journey can be called an *odyssey*.

Ancient Greece

Athletes today compete in the Olympic Games,
which were created by the ancient Greeks.

Olympic Athletes

The ancient Greeks greatly valued athletics, or skill and strength in physical sports. Training to be an athlete began when children were as^{25} young as seven years old.

Every four years, people from all over Greece gathered to watch athletes compete. These games were held in Olympia, a^{50} place in the countryside. Olympia was named after Mount Olympus, which was where the ancient Greeks believed their gods lived. The king of the gods^{75} was named Zeus.

The games were so important to the ancient Greeks that wars were stopped during the month before the games were held. This^{100} allowed athletes and visitors to travel safely to Olympia. Because the games were held in honor of the Greek god, Zeus, Olympic athletes were treated^{125} with honor. Even more honor was given to the people who won the games. Winners wore a wreath of olive branches and were believed to be like Zeus.^{153}

This plate shows a soldier from ancient Athens.

City-States

Greece has many mountains and islands, which can make travel difficult. In ancient times, people from different areas rarely met. Over time, certain[25] cities and the area around them became powerful city-states.

For many years, Athens and Sparta were Greece's most powerful city-states, although they differed[50] greatly. In Sparta, warriors were important. Children were trained to have strong bodies. In Athens, people with strong minds and bodies were important. Children learned[75] to play sports, but they also learned to read, write, and play music.

The ancient Greek city-states fought many wars. An especially long war[100] was fought between Athens and Sparta. Although Sparta won the war, both Athens and Sparta were weakened. Soon after the war, the city-state of[125] Macedonia conquered all of the Greek city-states, as well as lands beyond Greece. However, the armies of Rome conquered Macedonia less than 200 years later.[151]

REVIEW Ancient Greece

Write words that will help you remember what you learned.

The Ideas of Ancient Greece

_____

_____

_____

_____

Greek Myths

_____

_____

_____

_____

Greek Classics

_____

_____

_____

_____

Olympic Athletes

_____

_____

_____

_____

City-States

_____

_____

_____

_____

The Ideas of Ancient Greece

1. Greece is called "the birthplace of the Western world" because ___

   Ⓐ Greece is the oldest country in the world.

   Ⓑ Greece had the first government.

   Ⓒ Greek ideas influenced Western countries.

   Ⓓ Greece allowed everyone to be a citizen.

2. What kind of government did the ancient Greeks create?

   _____

   _____

   _____

Greek Myths

1. A myth is ___

   Ⓐ a story.

   Ⓑ a hero.

   Ⓒ a god or goddess.

   Ⓓ a writer or poet.

2. Retell what happened to Atlas in the Greek myth.

   _____

   _____

   _____

Greek Classics

1. What are the Greek classics?

    Ⓐ battles that were fought in ancient Greece

    Ⓑ important writers from ancient Greece

    Ⓒ myths that were written in ancient Greece

    Ⓓ ancient Greek literature that is important today

2. What are the *Iliad* and the *Odyssey*?

    _____

    _____

    _____

Olympic Athletes

1. Another good name for "Olympic Athletes" is ____

    Ⓐ "The Ancient Olympics."

    Ⓑ "Ancient Winners."

    Ⓒ "The Greek Gods."

    Ⓓ "Athletes From Mount Olympus."

2. Describe two ways you can tell that the Olympics were important to the ancient Greeks.

    _____

    _____

    _____

City-States

1. "City-States" is MAINLY about ___

   Ⓐ when Rome conquered Greece.

   Ⓑ powerful areas called city-states.

   Ⓒ how wars were fought in ancient Greece.

   Ⓓ the city-states of Rome and Greece.

2. How were Sparta and Athens different?

_____

_____

_____

Connect Your Ideas

1. Describe three things that were important to the ancient Greeks.

_____

_____

_____

2. What are two things the ancient Greeks created that exist today?

_____

_____

_____

The Depression Era

During the Great Depression, many people had to stand
in long lines to get food.

The Great Depression

Many Americans suffered during the Great Depression, which lasted from 1929 to 1940. Many lost their savings when the banks failed. In addition, many businesses closed, so people could not find work. But even those who did have jobs worked long hours and made so little money that they could barely feed themselves. Even young children worked so their family could eat.

During the Great Depression, many businesses were owned by people who did not care about workers' suffering. Owners kept wages low, paying as little as $5 each week. Even in the 1930s, this was not enough to live on.

Because so many people were suffering, workers began to demand more pay and fewer hours. They were largely ignored. At that time, many people believed that the U.S. government should stay out of people's daily lives. That belief began to change as more Americans suffered during the Great Depression.

The Depression Era

Crowds of people waited outside the New York Stock Exchange after the stock market crashed to see if they could get any of their money back.

The Stock Market

As they do today, people before the Great Depression bought and sold stocks on the stock market. When people own stock, they[25] own part of a company. People buy stocks because they think a company's profits will rise. People also hope to sell stocks for more than[50] they paid for them. For example, a stockowner who buys a stock for $20 and sells it for $30 makes $10.

Before the Great Depression,[75] people believed that stock prices would only rise. Businesses and banks also believed it was safe to make money by buying stocks.

In 1929, when[100] the stock market crashed, people who had bought stocks lost everything. Even people who had not bought stocks were hurt because the businesses closed that[125] they worked for. In addition, the banks closed, so people lost the money they had saved. In just a few weeks, more than a million Americans lost $30 billion.[154]

The Depression Era

A huge dust cloud blows toward a farm on the Great Plains.

The Dust Bowl

The United States had experienced droughts before the Great Depression. However, the drought in the Great Plains, which lasted from 1934 to[25] 1940, was particularly hard on the farms of the Midwest.

At that time, farmers did not know they should care for the topsoil. They planted[50] crops that did not help the soil hold water, and they cut down trees to make more farmland. Then, in 1934, very little rain fell[75] on the Great Plains, and strong winds blew. Because there were no trees to hold it, the wind carried the topsoil away. By the time[100] rain fell, there was no topsoil for planting crops.

Once a land of growing crops, the Great Plains became known as the Dust Bowl. More[125] than 2 1/2 million people left their farms in search of food and work. The little work they found could not end the hunger of the Great Depression.[153]

The Depression Era

During the Depression Era, families gathered in living rooms to listen to radio programs.

Low-Cost Entertainment

Although there was little money and food during the Great Depression, people entertained themselves in ways that cost very little or were [25] free. For example, people gathered in living rooms to listen to the radio. Children and adults listened to radio programs, like *The Lone Ranger* and [50] *The Shadow*. They also listened to sporting events, like baseball games and horse races.

Other low-cost forms of entertainment involved getting together with larger [75] groups of people. Some towns held weekly dances in barns or town centers. Local musicians played while people listened and danced. People also gathered to [100] play board or card games and to tell tall tales. These stories tried to make people's problems seem funny. One tall tale about the hot [125] weather was about a hen that laid hard-boiled eggs because it was so hot. These forms of entertainment helped take people's minds off their troubles. [151]

The Depression Era

As part of the New Deal, these men were hired to plant trees and create parks.

The New Deal

For the first four years of the Great Depression, the government did little to help people. Lawmakers, including President Hoover, believed that[25] the government should not interfere in people's daily life. Instead, President Hoover asked businesses to keep wages up and to hire more workers. Although he[50] believed that money would eventually reach people in need, it did not.

In 1932, Franklin Roosevelt was elected President of the United States. President Roosevelt[75] created a plan called the New Deal, which helped the people and the economy recover. President Roosevelt also started programs meant to prevent another Great[100] Depression.

President Roosevelt hired men to build parks. He also allowed the government to give money to banks. The banks then loaned the money to[125] people who wanted to buy homes. This practice helped banks stay in business. Finally, President Roosevelt reformed the stock market to make it safer for investing.[151]

The Depression Era

Write words that will help you remember what you learned.

The Great Depression

_____

_____

_____

_____

The Stock Market

_____

_____

_____

_____

The Dust Bowl

_____

_____

_____

_____

Low-Cost Entertainment

_____

_____

_____

_____

The New Deal

_____

_____

_____

_____

The Great Depression

1. During the Great Depression, ___

   Ⓐ the government failed.

   Ⓑ many people were out of work.

   Ⓒ many people moved to the United States.

   Ⓓ many people left the United States.

2. How did people's view of government begin to change during the Great Depression?

   _____

   _____

   _____

The Stock Market

1. Another good name for "The Stock Market" is ___

   Ⓐ "Stock Prices."

   Ⓑ "How Stock Markets Work."

   Ⓒ "Business in America."

   Ⓓ "The Stock Market Crash."

2. Describe two ways people lost money in the Great Depression.

   _____

   _____

   _____

The Dust Bowl

1. Why did the farmers leave their land during the Dust Bowl?

   Ⓐ They needed food and work.

   Ⓑ They went to buy topsoil for their farms.

   Ⓒ The rain flooded their farmland.

   Ⓓ They wanted to work in cities.

2. Why did the Midwest farmlands turn into the Dust Bowl?

   _____

   _____

   _____

Low-Cost Entertainment

1. During the Depression, people entertained themselves with ___

   Ⓐ television and radio.

   Ⓑ the Internet and movies.

   Ⓒ dancing and the radio.

   Ⓓ video games and dancing.

2. Why did people need low-cost entertainment during the Great Depression?

   _____

   _____

   _____

The New Deal

1. The New Deal helped the United States ___

   Ⓐ elect a new president.

   Ⓑ help the people of other countries.

   Ⓒ stay out of people's daily life.

   Ⓓ recover from the Great Depression.

2. How did the New Deal help people?

   _____

   _____

   _____

Connect Your Ideas

1. How did the Great Depression happen? What was one thing that helped end it?

   _____

   _____

   _____

2. Describe two ways in which life in the Depression Era differs from life today.

   _____

   _____

   _____

World War II

This picture shows German soldiers marching into Poland.

World War II Begins

On September 1, 1939, German military forces invaded Poland. Two days later, Britain and France declared war on Germany. The Second[25] World War had begun.

As the war went on, other nations joined the fighting. The Soviet Union joined when Germany attacked Soviet cities. The United[50] States joined when Japan attacked Pearl Harbor. Britain, France, the United States, and the Soviet Union fought together as the Allied forces. Nations that joined[75] Germany were called the Axis. The Axis nations included Germany, Italy, and Japan. Over the next six years, many nations around the world fought in[100] the war. It is estimated that 60 million soldiers and people who did not fight died during World War II.

Soon after World War II[125] began, Germany controlled most of Europe, including France. Italy controlled a few nations in northern Africa, and Japan controlled most of the nations in Southeast Asia.[151]

This World War II poster shows Rosie the Riveter building
a ship for the U.S. Navy.

The Home Front

In 1941, when the United States joined World War II, most Americans wanted to help the war effort. People covered holes in their old shoes with cardboard because rubber and cloth were needed to make soldiers' clothes. Children collected things that could be recycled, such as cans and paper. They also collected the fluff inside weed seeds, which was used in life jackets. Some children's groups, like the Boy Scouts and the Girl Scouts, sold billions of dollars in war stamps to help pay for the war.

The poster of Rosie the Riveter encouraged women to work for the war effort. It showed a woman riveting, or tightening, the bolts on a ship. Posters encouraged women to work in factories at home and to be nurses and pilots near the fighting. About six million women worked for the war effort, replacing the men who had gone to war.

World War II

American soldiers are shown landing on the beach at Normandy during the D-Day invasion.

D-Day

By 1944, the Allies were making progress against the Axis. Led by General Eisenhower, Allied military leaders planned Operation Overlord. The goals of Operation [25] Overlord included invading France at the beaches near Normandy and liberating France from Germany. The operation's final goal was to defeat Germany itself. The date [50] of the invasion was kept secret so it would be a surprise, so people called the invasion D-Day.

On June 6, 1944, at 12:15 A.M. [75], the D-Day invasion began with soldiers dropping onto the Normandy beaches from planes. Six hours later, American, British, and Canadian soldiers came ashore from ships. [100] In all, more than 156,000 Allied troops landed on the Normandy beaches. It is estimated that more than 5,000 Allied troops died during the D-Day [125] invasion.

The D-Day invasion was only the beginning of Operation Overlord. However, by the end of 1944, the Allied forces had liberated France from German control. [151]

World War II

This picture shows a group of men that have just been liberated from a German work camp.

The War on People

Some groups of people suffered more than others during World War II. Many were killed because of their[25] skin color.

Germany's leader, Adolph Hitler, decided to blame some groups for the nation's problems. Adolph Hitler sent to work camps people of the Jewish[50] faith, children of mixed race, and people with disabilities. An estimated six million men, women, and children died or were killed in these camps.

After[75] Japan attacked Pearl Harbor, many Americans on the mainland feared that they would be attacked, too. They thought that Japanese Americans who lived in the[100] United States were spying for the enemy. Although there was no proof that they were spies, more than 120,000 Japanese Americans were taken from their[125] homes and forced to live in prison camps in the western United States. Even though many were American citizens, they lost their jobs, their homes, and their rights.[153]

World War II

The cloud was produced by the atomic bomb that was dropped on Nagasaki. The other picture shows the damage the bomb caused.

The End of World War II

For six years, World War II continued around the world. British, Canadian, and American troops fought German troops from[25] the west, while Soviet troops attacked Germany from the east. When the Soviet Union invaded the capital of Germany, Adolph Hitler killed himself. Soon after,[50] on May 8, 1945, Germany surrendered. World War II had ended in Europe.

However, even though Germany surrendered, World War II was still being fought[75] in Asia. Both Japanese and American troops suffered great losses, although neither side would surrender.

Then, the United States used a new kind of powerful[100] bomb, called an atomic bomb. In August 1945, the United States dropped atomic bombs on both Hiroshima and Nagasaki, Japan. An estimated 100,000 people were[125] either killed or missing in Hiroshima and Nagasaki as a result of these bombs. On August 14, 1945, Japan surrendered. World War II had ended.[150]

 **World War II**

Write words that will help you remember what you learned.

World War II Begins

_____

_____

_____

_____

The Home Front

_____

_____

_____

_____

D-Day

_____

_____

_____

_____

The War on People

_____

_____

_____

_____

The End of World War II

_____

_____

_____

_____

World War II Begins

1. "World War II Begins" is MAINLY about ___

   Ⓐ the United States in World War II.

   Ⓑ who fought in World War II.

   Ⓒ the Axis nations.

   Ⓓ why Germany went to war.

2. When did the United States begin fighting in World War II?

   _____

   _____

   _____

The Home Front

1. "The Home Front" is MAINLY about ___

   Ⓐ the places where the armies fought.

   Ⓑ how people at home helped the war effort.

   Ⓒ U.S. factories that helped the war effort.

   Ⓓ how the United States paid for the war.

2. Describe three ways people in the United States worked for the war.

   _____

   _____

   _____

D-Day

1. What was D-Day?

   Ⓐ the date the United States was invaded

   Ⓑ when World War II ended

   Ⓒ the date an invasion of France began

   Ⓓ the beginning of World War II

2. What was Operation Overlord?

   _____

   _____

   _____

The War on People

1. The main idea of "The War on People" is that ___

   Ⓐ Adolph Hitler killed many Japanese Americans.

   Ⓑ people who were not soldiers also suffered during the war.

   Ⓒ American soldiers suffered during the war.

   Ⓓ people who were not soldiers helped the war effort at home.

2. What happened to Japanese Americans in the United States during World War II?

   _____

   _____

   _____

The End of World War II

1. How did World War II end in Europe?

   Ⓐ Hitler attacked the Soviet Union.

   Ⓑ Japan surrendered.

   Ⓒ The atomic bomb was dropped.

   Ⓓ Germany surrendered.

2. What event ended World War II in Asia?

   _____

   _____

   _____

Connect Your Ideas

1. How did World War II start? How did it end?

   _____

   _____

   _____

2. Describe two ways the war affected people who did not fight.

   _____

   _____

   _____

The Scientific Method

Observing is the first step in the scientific method.

What Is the Scientific Method?

People gather information about many things, such as where to travel or what to buy. Some families even keep records[25] about which television to buy based on price, size, or picture quality.

When scientists want to understand something, they also gather information. The four steps[50] they use for gathering information are called the scientific method.

In Step One of the scientific method, a scientist observes something, such as when plants[75] bloom. A scientist who observes that some plants bloom at night might ask why this happens. In Step Two, the scientist uses the observation to[100] create a possible explanation, called a hypothesis. In Step Three, the scientist uses the hypothesis to make a prediction. In Step Four, the scientist carries[125] [3] out experiments to test the prediction. The results of the experiments tell the scientist if the prediction was accurate or if a different hypothesis needs to be tested.[153]

The Scientific Method

Jane Goodall observed chimpanzees and made notes about what she saw.

The Study of Animals

The scientific method can be used in many different settings, even in jungles with wild animals. In 1960, little was known[25] about chimpanzees. The scientist Jane Goodall decided to study them in their natural habitat in Africa, instead of in a zoo.

Jane Goodall observed chimpanzees[50] in the jungles of Africa for many years. She watched them gather food, make nests, and take care of each other. She also made detailed[75] notes of her observations to help her remember exactly what she saw.

Jane Goodall used her observations to make many hypotheses and predictions about chimpanzees.[100] She then tested her predictions by collecting new observations, taking more notes, and studying these notes.

By observing chimpanzees in their natural habitat, Jane Goodall[125] made many discoveries. One discovery was that chimpanzees could solve certain kinds of problems. Knowing that they could solve problems changed how people think about chimpanzees.[151]

The Scientific Method

Thomas Edison stands next to a model of his first light bulb and holds a newer model of the bulb in his hand.

The Study of Light Bulbs

The scientist Thomas Edison thought he could invent a light bulb that would glow for a long time. To invent[25] such a bulb, he experimented with bulbs of different shapes and sizes. Finally, Edison made the hypothesis that it was the small wire, or filament,[50] inside the bulb that changed how long the bulb glowed. Edison tried more than 1,000 filaments made of different materials. Finally, in 1879, he discovered[75] a filament that glowed for a long time.

In each experiment, Thomas Edison manipulated, or changed, one part of the light bulb. Whatever can be[100] manipulated in an experiment is called a variable. Some of the variables Edison manipulated were the size and shape of the bulb and the material[125] of the filament. Scientists try to manipulate one variable at a time in their experiments. In this way, they know which variable made a difference.[150]

The Scientific Method

Scientists must test a hypothesis to see if it is correct
or if it needs to be changed.

Scientific Experiments

Scientists can only say that they proved a prediction if their experiment was fair. A fair experiment is one in which everything but[25] the variable is the same from one test to another. In addition, everything that happens must be fairly observed.

For example, a scientist might make[50] the hypothesis that a plant would grow better in strong daylight than in weak daylight. To test this hypothesis, the scientist would plant two sets[75] of seeds. Then, the scientist would make sure that everything is the same for both sets of seeds, except the amount of daylight they receive.[100] The seeds would be planted at the same time, in the same depth of soil, and in the same kind of soil. The seeds would[125] also get the same amount of water. When everything except the amount of daylight is the same for both sets of seeds, the hypothesis has been fairly tested.[153]

The Scientific Method

In this picture, a bat flies near some evening primrose flowers.

Fact and Theory

It is a scientific fact that the evening primrose, a plant that lives in the desert, blooms at night. This scientific fact[25] was accepted because scientists carefully observed the evening primrose in the desert.

A theory is an explanation of how or why something happens. A scientific[50] theory is an explanation that is supported by experiments that have been done many times. Scientific theories change when new experiments fail to support them,[75] but these theories explain scientists' best ideas about how things work.

Germ theory is one example of a scientific theory. About 150 years ago, a[100] French scientist did many experiments to find out why people got sick. He found that some diseases are caused by bacteria. The scientist repeated his[125] experiments many times until he was sure that bacteria caused those illnesses. In proving the germ theory, the scientist helped others find ways to cure illnesses caused by germs.[154]

 **The Scientific Method**

Write words that will help you remember what you learned.

What Is the Scientific Method?

_____

_____

_____

_____

The Study of Animals

_____

_____

_____

_____

The Study of Light Bulbs

_____

_____

_____

_____

Scientific Experiments

_____

_____

_____

_____

Fact and Theory

_____

_____

_____

_____

What Is the Scientific Method?

1. The scientific method is ___

    Ⓐ a way to teach science to students.

    Ⓑ the steps used for gathering information.

    Ⓒ a hypothesis for why things happen.

    Ⓓ the experiments needed to test predictions.

2. Describe the scientific method.

_____

_____

_____

The Study of Animals

1. The main idea of this reading is that ___

    Ⓐ chimpanzees learn by observing each other.

    Ⓑ scientists observe so they can make hypotheses.

    Ⓒ observations are based on discoveries.

    Ⓓ observations can help scientists learn.

2. How did Jane Goodall learn about chimpanzees?

_____

_____

_____

The Study of Light Bulbs

1. A variable is ___

    Ⓐ something that changes.

    Ⓑ a kind of experiment.

    Ⓒ something that can be proved.

    Ⓓ one way to test a hypothesis.

2. How did Thomas Edison invent a light bulb that glowed for a long time?

    _____

    _____

    _____

Scientific Experiments

1. "Scientific Experiments" is MAINLY about how to set up ___

    Ⓐ the right number of variables.

    Ⓑ fair hypotheses.

    Ⓒ experiments that can be tested.

    Ⓓ fair experiments.

2. How can a scientist set up a fair experiment?

    _____

    _____

    _____

Fact and Theory

1. A scientific fact is ___

   Ⓐ a theory based on a hypothesis.

   Ⓑ a prediction about what will happen.

   Ⓒ an explanation of a theory.

   Ⓓ an idea that has been accepted.

2. What is germ theory?

   _____

   _____

   _____

Connect Your Ideas

1. Describe how two scientists in these readings used the scientific method.

   _____

   _____

   _____

2. Why is it important to set up a fair experiment?

   _____

   _____

   _____

Constructing a Building

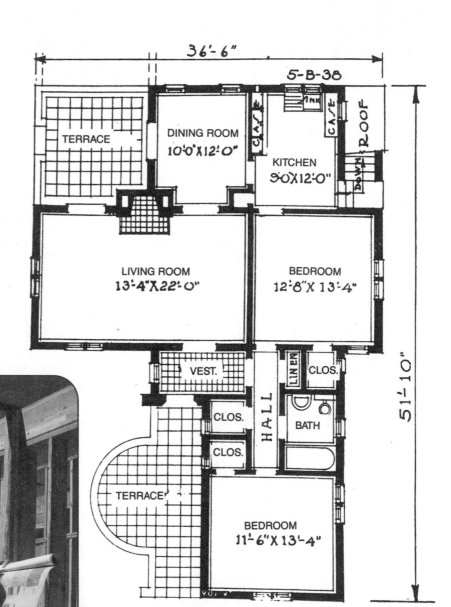

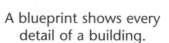

A blueprint shows every
detail of a building.

Beginning With a Blueprint

Construction of a building begins with a blueprint. Blueprints are detailed scale drawings of a building. Scale refers to the ratio[25] between the drawing and the real building. In blueprints for houses, the ratio between the drawing and the real building is usually a quarter inch[50] to one foot. That means that a bedroom of 10 feet by 12 feet will measure 2.5 inches by 3 inches on a blueprint.

The[75] experts who design buildings are called architects. Architects design every detail of a building. Their blueprints show the exact size and location of every room,[100] door, and window. Blueprints also show where the light switches, water pipes, and heating ducts will be.

At one time, final blueprints were printed in[125] a special way. The architect's design was shown in white print on blue paper. Although plans are no longer printed in this way, architects' designs are still called blueprints.[154]

Constructing a Building

Every building needs a good foundation to make it safe and strong.

A Firm Foundation

Roots are needed to support the weight of a tree. Similarly, a strong foundation is needed to support a building. Without a [25] strong foundation, a building can shift over time. Floors can sag and walls can crack in buildings with weak foundations.

Before they choose the kind [50] of foundation they will use, architects think about the climate near the house. In places with freezing winters, like the American Midwest, home construction begins [75] with a deep hole. The concrete walls and floor of the foundation are poured into the hole. This kind of foundation also creates a basement, [100] or cellar.

In mild climates, like Florida or California, foundations are still made of concrete. However, the concrete is often poured into a shallow trench. [125] The concrete makes a low wall that outlines the shape of the house. In earthquake-prone areas, metal bars are put into the concrete to strengthen the foundation. [153]

Constructing a Building

A roof keeps the people and things in a house safe from the sun and rain.

Supporting the Roof

A roof protects the people and things inside a house from the weather. Typically, but not always, a roof slopes down from[25] a ridge so that rain will run off. In places that get a lot of snow, the slope of a roof must be steep enough[50] to keep the snow from getting too thick. A roof must be designed to bear its own weight, as well as the weight of any[75] water, ice, or snow that stays on it. Water and snow are heavy, though, so too much of either one can damage a roof.

Most[100] roofs are built by placing wooden or metal structures on top of the walls of the house. These wooden or metal structures make a strong[125] framework for the roof. Boards are then attached to this framework. Finally, roof tiles are attached to the boards to create the surface of the roof.[151]

Constructing a Building

This drawing shows how a U-trap is connected to a sink.

Drains and Vents

Water that goes down the drains of sinks, tubs, showers, and toilets is called wastewater. Wastewater may contain bacteria that produce unwanted[25] or dangerous gases. U-traps keep these dangerous gases from getting back into a house.

A U-trap is a bend in a pipe that looks like[50] the letter *U*. Located directly under every sink, tub, shower, and toilet, a U-trap traps wastewater in the bottom of the *U*. The water in[75] the U-trap acts as a barrier, preventing dangerous gases from escaping into the house.

Although U-traps are useful, they can also cause problems. Over time,[100] gases can bubble up through the water in the U-trap and escape into the house. The solution is to add a small pipe, called a[125] vent, that branches off the drain pipe just below the U-trap. The vent lets the gases rise to the roof, where they can safely escape.[150]

Constructing a Building

The solar panels on this roof collect energy from the Sun.

Zero-Energy Homes

Many builders today use strategies that reduce the amount of electricity a home uses. Such homes are called zero-energy homes because[25] they use very little energy.

One strategy for building a zero-energy home is to use very efficient heaters and air conditioners. Water can also[50] be heated when it is needed, rather than keeping a full tank of hot water at all times. Another strategy is to build a free[75] energy source, like solar or wind power, into the house.

A zero-energy strategy should be chosen with the area's climate and weather patterns in[100] mind. For example, zero-energy homes in cold climates have outside walls and a roof that lose very little heat. Extra material is also added[125] to the walls and ceilings, special windows keep heat in, and windows face the Sun. All of these strategies reduce the amount of energy a home uses.[152]

Constructing a Building

Write words that will help you remember what you learned.

Beginning With a Blueprint

_____

_____

_____

_____

A Firm Foundation

_____

_____

_____

_____

Supporting the Roof

_____

_____

_____

_____

Drains and Vents

_____

_____

_____

_____

Zero-Energy Homes

_____

_____

_____

_____

Beginning With a Blueprint

1. What is a blueprint?

   Ⓐ a plan of a building

   Ⓑ a kind of paper architects use

   Ⓒ the size of a house

   Ⓓ a way to design a building

2. What do blueprints show?

   _____

   _____

   _____

A Firm Foundation

1. What does a foundation do?

   Ⓐ It makes a building's floors sag.

   Ⓑ It supports a building.

   Ⓒ It makes the climate mild near a building.

   Ⓓ It creates a shallow trench.

2. Why do buildings need strong foundations?

   _____

   _____

   _____

Constructing a Building

Supporting the Roof

1. "Supporting the Roof" is MAINLY about ___

   Ⓐ how roofs are built.

   Ⓑ materials used to build roofs.

   Ⓒ why roofs have slopes.

   Ⓓ different kinds of roofs.

2. How can rain or snow damage a roof?

   _____

   _____

   _____

Drains and Vents

1. What do vent pipes do?

   Ⓐ They move dangerous gases out of a house.

   Ⓑ They vent gases into the U-trap.

   Ⓒ They keep sinks from stopping up.

   Ⓓ They take wastewater out of a house.

2. How do U-traps work?

   _____

   _____

   _____

Zero-Energy Homes

1. Zero-energy homes are homes that ___
   - (A) are built in warm climates.
   - (B) use very little energy.
   - (C) have the same strategy in all climates.
   - (D) use only electric power.

2. Describe a zero-energy strategy.

   _____

   _____

   _____

Connect Your Ideas

1. What are two important things to include when building a house?

   _____

   _____

   _____

2. Suppose there was another reading in this topic. Do you think it would be about painting a home or building a garage? Why?

   _____

   _____

   _____

Computers

People today can read, write, and shop on computers.

What Is a Computer?

A computer is a machine that can be programmed to do mathematical and logical tasks. Computers organize, process, and store information.[25] However, because computers are changing quickly, this description may not be useful for very long.

Computers can do a wide variety of tasks at lightning[50] speed. They can carry out huge numbers of calculations in one second. They can be used to create, edit, and store books, music, and movies.[75] Before computers were invented, people wrote everything by hand or with typewriters. Writing by hand or with typewriters did not allow people to change their[100] work easily. Computers, however, allow writers to change a few words or a whole paragraph in only a few seconds.

Computers can also communicate with[125] each other over long or short distances. This feature makes it possible for people to send words, music, and pictures around the world in just a few seconds.[153]

Computers

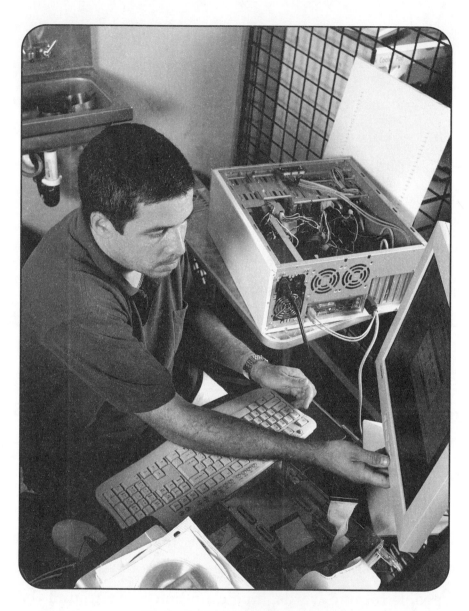

Computers are filled with wires and other components that process and store information.

What's Inside a Computer?

Most computers contain several components, or pieces. They have a processor, memory, and input/output devices, plus the wiring that connects [25] all of these parts. The processor calculates and makes logical decisions. Memory stores the data and the instructions for what the processor is supposed to [50] do with the data. Input devices, like a mouse or a keyboard, allow users to tell the computer what to do. Output devices, like a [75] screen or a printer, show the user what the computer has done.

Most computers have two kinds of memory devices. Information that is needed often [100] and quickly is stored on memory chips. These chips have no moving parts and store small amounts of data. Larger amounts of data are usually [125] stored on a hard drive, a compact disc (CD), or a digital video disc (DVD). Compact discs, digital video discs, and hard drives are all known as computer hardware. [154]

Computers

The software on the computers helps students do math problems.

Software

Computer hardware, such as compact discs and hard drives, is useless without computer software. Software controls what happens inside a computer. A set of [25] instructions for a task is called a program. People who write programs are called programmers. Several computer languages have been developed for writing software. Each [50] one has its own symbols and grammar. For a computer to do a task, the software for that task must be in the same language [75] as the software that runs the computer.

There are two types of computer software. The first is system software, which manages the computer's hardware. It [100] also does tasks like moving data into memory and showing words on a screen. System software acts like an umbrella, allowing applications to operate underneath [125] it.

The other type of software, called application software, does specific tasks, like processing words or playing music. Application software usually works under the umbrella of the system software. [154]

Computers

Software can be used to work, to learn, and to play games.

Software Development

When you use a computer to complete a task, you are using software that was designed for that task. Although people can learn[25] computer languages and use them to write programs, most people buy software in stores or download software from the Internet. Commercial software, like word-processing[50] programs and games, is very complicated. A single program may have thousands of instructions.

Commercial software is created by teams of people that use a[75] software development process. First, the program is broken down into parts. Then, sections of the program, called routines, are written for each part.

The development[100] process includes tests for each part of the software. Once each part is complete, the parts are combined to create the program. Errors in programs[125] are called bugs. The process of finding and fixing bugs is called debugging. The development of a complicated software program may take several years and involve many programmers.[153]

Computers

Computer networks let people send pictures and messages
quickly around the world.

Computer Networks

Early computers worked on their own. However, it was not long before two computers were connected, forming a simple network.

In 1968, an[25] early form of the Internet was created when three computers in California and one in Utah were connected. In 1981, a plan was created that[50] would connect many different networks. This was the beginning of the Internet. Network speeds grew quickly, and many people began to use them. By 1996,[75] about seven million computers were connected to the Internet.

As the Internet grew, it became difficult for users to find all of the information that[100] was stored on Web pages around the world. Lycos, the first search engine, was developed in 1993. It kept track of about 800,000 Web pages.[125] By November 2004, the Google search engine was searching more than eight billion Web pages. Today, the Internet continues to expand as new hardware and software are created.[153]

Computers

Write words that will help you remember what you learned.

What Is a Computer?

_____

_____

_____

_____

What's Inside a Computer?

_____

_____

_____

_____

Software

_____

_____

_____

_____

Software Development

_____

_____

_____

_____

Computer Networks

_____

_____

_____

_____

What Is a Computer?

1. The main idea of "What Is a Computer?" is that ___

   Ⓐ computers are used by many people today.

   Ⓑ computers help us do many things.

   Ⓒ computers are difficult to understand.

   Ⓓ computers will be more useful in the future.

2. Describe one way computers have changed the way people do things.

   _____

   _____

   _____

What's Inside a Computer?

1. Another good name for "What's Inside a Computer?" is ___

   Ⓐ "How to Use a Computer."

   Ⓑ "Inventing Computers."

   Ⓒ "The Parts of a Computer."

   Ⓓ "Changes in Computers."

2. Name three components of a computer.

   _____

   _____

   _____

Software

1. What is software?

   (A) instructions that control what happens in a computer

   (B) the parts of a computer that work together

   (C) the languages that computer programmers use

   (D) how a computer system does its tasks

2. What is the difference between system software and application software?

   _____

   _____

   _____

Software Development

1. "Software Development" is MAINLY about ___

   (A) how to create computer hardware.

   (B) how to use computer programs.

   (C) how computer programs are created.

   (D) how to debug commercial software.

2. How is commercial software created?

   _____

   _____

   _____

Computer Networks

1. Which of the following BEST describes a computer network?

    Ⓐ people who trade stories about computers

    Ⓑ the software and hardware on a computer

    Ⓒ companies that make computers

    Ⓓ computers that work together

2. How did networks change the way people used computers?

    _____

    _____

Connect Your Ideas

1. What is the difference between computer hardware and software?

    _____

    _____

    _____

2. How are early computers different from the computers of today?

    _____

    _____

    _____

Reading Log • Level F • Book 3

	I Read This	New Words I Learned	New Facts I Learned	What Else I Want to Learn About This Subject
Ancient Greece				
The Ideas of Ancient Greece				
Greek Myths				
Greek Classics				
Olympic Athletes				
City-States				
The Depression Era				
The Great Depression				
The Stock Market				
The Dust Bowl				
Low-Cost Entertainment				
The New Deal				
World War II				
World War II Begins				
The Home Front				
D-Day				
The War on People				
The End of World War II				

	I Read This	New Words I Learned	New Facts I Learned	What Else I Want to Learn About This Subject
The Scientific Method				
What Is the Scientific Method?				
The Study of Animals				
The Study of Light Bulbs				
Scientific Experiments				
Fact and Theory				
Constructing a Building				
Beginning With a Blueprint				
A Firm Foundation				
Supporting the Roof				
Drains and Vents				
Zero-Energy Homes				
Computers				
What Is a Computer?				
What's Inside a Computer?				
Software				
Software Development				
Computer Networks				

Self-Check Graph

	The Ideas of Ancient Greece	Greek Myths	Greek Classics	Olympic Athletes	City-States	The Great Depression	The Stock Market	The Dust Bowl	Low-Cost Entertainment	The New Deal	World War II Begins	The Home Front	D-Day	The War on People	The End of World War II	What Is the Scientific Method?	The Study of Animals	The Study of Light Bulbs	Scientific Experiments	Fact and Theory	Beginning With a Blueprint	A Firm Foundation	Supporting the Roof	Drains and Vents	Zero-Energy Homes	What Is a Computer?	What's Inside a Computer?	Software	Software Development	Computer Networks
160																														
158																														
156																														
154																														
152																														
150																														
148																														
146																														
144																														
142																														
140																														
138																														
136																														
134																														
132																														
130																														
128																														
126																														
124																														
122																														
120																														
118																														
116																														
114																														
112																														
110																														
108																														
106																														
104																														
102																														
100																														
98																														
96																														
94																														
92																														
90																														
88																														
86																														
84																														
82																														
80																														